Creating A Garden Wildlife Pond

Contents

A Place Of Wonder

The sun creeps above the horizon, bathing the yellow flag plants with warmth and light, as an ugly-looking creature crawls slowly from the depths of the pond. It stops some 12 inches (30 cms) above the water surface, its six legs tightly grasping the flag stem. Slowly the skin splits along its back, and the head and thorax of an insect emerges to grasp the case with its new legs, before pulling its abdomen clear.

After resting for a while, the milky wings start to expand as fluid is pumped in and the insect crawls further up the flag stem to catch the warmth of the early morning sun. Its wings, held at 90 degrees to its body, harden and become transparent; less than four hours from when the nymph left the water, it has been transformed into a beautiful dragonfly.

The dragonfly nymph climbs a plant stem and the case splits.

Once the dragonfly has squeezed out, the wings open and harden in the early morning sun.

Why Build A Wildlife Pond?

A garden wildlife pond is home to many creatures that come to rely on it for a place to drink and bathe throughout the year. As spring approaches, it teems with activity, as many creatures (which can live happily on the land for most of the time) move in to breed.

The wildlife pond is the hub of the wildlife garden. A successful pond will go a long way towards ensuring that your wild flower meadow bristles with life, your nest boxes are occupied, and, most importantly, the rich diversity of life present in the garden ensures that your fruit, flowers and vegetables are not overrun with pests.

Apart from the benefit to wildlife and the garden as a whole, your wildlife pond will become a source of interest throughout the year as you watch nature in action.

A wildlife pond will attract a wide variety of creatures to your garden, and will give you hours of pleasure.

First Steps

The ideal wildlife pond is lined with natural clay.

The best wildlife pond will be the one which is most like a natural pond – lined with puddled clay, a thick layer of natural clay which is worked with the feet to form a water-tight membrane. Although good fun, it is a long, expensive and difficult job which is not always successful, so most ponds are fitted with a flexible liner. A medium-quality liner should remain watertight for 15 to 25 years.

Generally, the pond should be as large as possible, but its dimensions will obviously be limited by the size of your garden.

Before starting to dig, consider these points.

1 Keep the shape simple. Round or oval will make it much easier to fit the liner.

2 Getting the right profile is just as important as maximizing the surface area. Make sure there are shallow areas, wide flat shelves at different depths, and an area that is at least three feet (91 cms) deep to provide winter protection.

3 Choose a site that will receive between five and eight hours of sunshine each day.

4 Do not build your pond directly under trees – the leaves will contaminate the water and the roots may puncture the liner.

Building The Pond

1 Having selected a suitable site, mark out the proposed shape using sand or a length of hosepipe.

2 Remove the top layer. If it is turf, then stack it to one side, as it will be useful later.

3 Dig out the soil to create a hole with shallows, shelves, and a deep area.

4 Knock in some pegs around the perimeter, and, using a length of timber and a spirit level, make sure the pegs are all level. Using the turf, you can build up any low places, and, with a spade, reduce any high spots so that all the pegs are a couple of inches above the pond perimeter. It is important to get this stage right as it will determine how much liner shows above the water level, as well as maximising the volume of water in the pond.

5 Using a length of timber and a rule, check the depth of the pond and dig out more soil if necessary. Then smooth the surface and remove any stones or other sharp objects.

Use sand to mark out the shape of your pond.

Cut out the turf and stack it on polythene for later use.

Set the different pond levels by using pegs.

Building The Pond

Remove sharp stones and rake in the sand, before laying down an old carpet.

Place the liner over the hole, and use a hose pipe to fill it with water.

6 Line the inside of the hole with at least 1 inch (2.5 cms) of sand, followed by a layer of old carpet or any material which will protect the liner.

7 Measure up for the liner. You will need to know the maximum length, width and depth of the pond. The amount you will need is obtained from the formula: L + 2D x W + 2D. Liner is purchased off a roll, so you can have any length you want, but you will be limited to standard widths unless you pay extra to have pieces joined. So it makes sense to familiarise yourself with the sizes available before digging the hole.

8 Spread the liner out on a flat surface, ideally on a warm day, so that any creases in the liner disappear as it warms up. Then gently position the liner over the hole, ensuring that the overlap is even all round, and hold it in position with a few large stones placed round the edge.

9 Slowly start to fill the pond with water from a hosepipe until the deepest part of the pond is full. This will ensure a snug fit for the liner, preventing it from moving while it is smoothed into place round the edge of the pond.

10 Cover the liner with 2 inches (5 cms) of sieved subsoil (which is low in nutrients) and firm it down, before continuing to fill the pond with water to within three inches (7.5 cms) of the top.

Cut away the surplus liner at the edges, then hold down the edge with the turves.

11 Using scissors, cut away any surplus liner, leaving approximately 12 inches (30 cms) round the edge, which is then secured by burying it under the soil or trapping it under a layer of turf placed round the perimeter.

The finished results after eight weeks (above) and two years (below).

12 Continue to fill the pond until the water level is within an inch (2.5 cms) of over-flowing from the pond. Finally, leave the pond for at least a week before you think about planting.

Plants: The Powerhouse

A healthy, well-planted pond is your first step to achieving a habitat that is teeming with life.

Most people are keen to introduce amphibians to their new pond, but it is much better to concentrate on the planting – and then the native wildlife will surely follow. By planting a variety of native plants in and around the pond, you will create a healthy and varied pond habitat – a habitat that, with a little help, will remain balanced and continue to function year after year.

In Deep Water

Pond plants can be conveniently divided into four groups, all of which have specific functions to perform. Let's start with the deep-water plants. These are often referred to as oxygenators because, in the presence of sunlight, their underwater leaves take in carbon dioxide (which is poisonous to animal life) and produce oxygen, which is essential for their well-being. Unfortunately, the situation is reversed at night, when they take up oxygen, although this is only likely to be a problem in a very overcrowded pond.

Restrict yourself to two or three species because oxygenators will grow very quickly and can easily take over the pond. There is plenty of choice, including hornwort, water crowfoot, water starwort, willow moss, water violet and curled pondweed.

Canadian pondweed is found in many small ponds, but avoid plants like chara and the alien Australian stonecrop (often sold as Tilia recurva), both of which will form thick, impenetrable mats at the expense of other plants.

Usually sold in bunches by garden centres, oxygenators stand the best chance if rooted in a planter containing a pond-soil mixture and gently lowered into the deeper part of the pond.

Water crowfoot is a successful – and attractive – deep-water oxygenator.

Plants: The Powerhouse

Floaters

Floaters are plants which either float freely at or near the surface (like the water soldier and duckweed), or are anchored to the bottom but produce large floating leaves (like the water lily and arrowhead).

They have an important part to play in the pond's stability by excluding light from the water, which helps to prevent algae growing too quickly and turning the water green, red or brown.

True floaters are easy to plant – simply drop them into the water– but avoid some of the aliens, like azolla, which can cover the whole surface in a few weeks, shutting out the light.

Other aliens include: water lettuce, water hyacinth, and water chestnut. Water lilies must be established in soil if they are to thrive.

The water lily is one of the most popular of all pond floater plants.

Avoid azolla which will cover the entire pond, starving it of light, in a matter of weeks.

Shallow Levels

As we move closer to the bank, we come across a group of plants which grow best in shallow water where their roots gain a foothold in the mud. These plants help to keep the nutrient levels under control, as too much nutrient can lead to an explosion of algal or floater (e.g. duckweed) growth.

Monkey musk, spearwort, marestail and water forget-me-not all come into this category, but watch out for the alien marsh pennywort.

Place the plants in groups in planters, which can be located on a shelf covered with about 6 inches (15 cms) of water.

Water forget-me-not grows best in shallow water.

Marginals

Finally, we come to the marginals, those plants which need plenty of water but which need their roots firmly bedded into the soil. Here the choice is larger, as the smaller plants, like marsh marigold, brooklime and bogbean, compete with the larger reed maces, yellow flags and loosestrifes for the pond edge.

Rushes and grasses also come into their own here, as well as some of the more delicate flowers, like the ladies' smock and marsh orchids.

Bog bean is a popular marginal plant.

Colonisation Begins

A quick swim by a pair of mallards can introduce plants such as duckweed.

Build a pond, fill it with water, and even before any plants have been introduced – let alone had time to establish – colonisation begins.

A pair of mallards arrive for an exploratory swim, leaving behind a few pieces of duckweed. These will remain on the surface, probably drifting in the wind to a sheltered corner, and then, when conditions are right, will grow rapidly, capable of covering the surface in a season.

Insect Invasion

Notonecta the backswimmer appears, hanging motionless in the water, having flown from a nearby pond. Water beetles, including the large great diving beetle, are also good fliers, seeking out new ponds in the spring where they can lay their eggs.

As summer arrives, other insects fly in to visit, and some will stop to lay their eggs. Common darters dip into the water, while larger southern hawkers lay their eggs in the mud around the edge.

The backswimmer hangs upside down in the water, waiting for its prey.

The Tinies

A small bucket full of sludge from a neighbouring pond introduces many of the microscopic creatures necessary for the well-being of the pond.

Bloodworms, daphnia, mosquito larvae, and bacteria, which are responsible for the breakdown of harmful ammonia into nitrites and nitrates, will all be present.

Mosquito larvae rest below the surface of the water so they can breathe air.

Plant Life

Another source of animal life is the plants we introduce. Clinging to the leaves and hiding among the roots will be leaches, dragonfly and damselfly nymphs, beetle larvae, mayfly nymphs, caddis grubs, snails and their eggs, and many more.

Amphibian Landings

Even in the first year, it is not unusual for a few common frogs to turn up and produce a few handfuls of spawn. Once they start, they will return in greater numbers each year.

Newts – common, palmate and even the great crested – appear as if from nowhere to breed in the spring, while birds and mammals will use the new-found supply of water for drinking and bathing.

Within two years the natural cycle will be established and your pond will be self-perpetuating year after year.

With a healthy insect population in the pond, it won't be long before newts and other amphibians move in.

On The Surface

W̲hy is the pond such a popular place for living creatures? Almost without exception, they need water simply to survive, but they have adapted to exploit every part of the pond, and there are even insects which have made the surface their home.

Pond Skaters

The pond skater has a hairy pad on the bottom of each foot, which gives it additional buoyancy, preventing it from breaking through the surface film and allowing it to skate over the surface at great speed.

The much smaller and more delicate water measurer (*Hydrometra stagporum*) is also found on the surface, together with the water cricket, hiding among the floating plants.

The pondskater's hairy pads on the bottom of its feet allows him to walk on water!

Whirly Gigs

A creature which is much more obvious on the surface is the whirly gig beetle. These tiny beetles are often found in large numbers as they whiz round and round at great speed on the surface, stopping occasionally before taking off again on their haphazard journey.

Back Swimmer

The back swimmer, which is about an inch (2.5 cms) long, is another creature which has adapted to life on the surface, although, if danger threatens, it can dive quickly under the water. Its back legs have been extended and adapted so that they are just like a pair of oars, while its back has become keel-shaped, allowing it to row quickly through the water.

The backswimmer appears harmless, but, to other insects, it is a skilled and deadly predator.

Armed with a beak-like rostrum (snout), this water bug waits patiently on the surface; when an insect falls into the water, it senses the vibrations caused by the insect's struggles and moves in for the kill. It pierces the insect with its sharp rostrum, injecting a liquid which kills the insect and starts to dissolve its body. The backswimmer then sucks out the contents, leaving a hollow shell.

Coming Up For Air

Other creatures utilise the surface, because, while they like to remain submerged, they also need to breathe air. If you look into a water butt in summer, you may notice movement as the mosquito larvae dive.

Rat-tailed maggots feed on the pond bottom and send up long breathing tubes to the surface.

Wait patiently and soon they start to return to the surface, where they rest with their spiracles (air tubes) just breaking the surface. The rat-tailed maggot rests on the bottom, where it feeds, and sends up an extendible tube through which it can take in air.

Amphibian Invasion

Every spring, the common frog emerges from hibernation and treks to the pond from which it hatched.

As the days lengthen, winter makes way for spring, triggering one of nature's annual marvels. From under logpiles, stones, small holes in the bank, and even from the depths of the pond itself, the common frog stirs, responding to the warmer weather.

Their winter hibernation at an end, the frogs make their way unerringly towards their chosen breeding site, the pond where, three or four years earlier, they hatched. The males, which outnumber the females, arrive first to grab a female as soon as she enters the water.

Croaky Chorus

At the height of the breeding season, the noise of a large number of amphibians, all croaking in an effort to attract a mate, can be heard from all parts of the garden. Towards the middle of the pond, anchored to, and partially covering, the water plants is a large mass of transparent jelly. A closer look reveals that it is frog spawn, made up of thousands of tiny spheres of jelly, each containing a small black central dot.

Stand motionless beside the pond and in less than three minutes a head pops up out of the water, partially hidden behind some weed. Then another and another, and within five minutes there are more than 50 heads showing above the water. The croaking starts slowly but gradually increases as more heads become visible.

Mating Game

Some of the frogs move out of the water to scramble over the mass of spawn, while others move through the water in search of a mate, presumably attracted by the croaking. Males outnumber females, and the competition for a mate is intense. Often three or more males will converge on the same female, all trying to grasp the female from behind in a grip known as amplexus.

Once clasped, it is very difficult to break this grip and the pair remain motionless in the water, the female retaining her buoyancy by resting her feet on a piece of weed. The male will not release his grip until spawning is completed

The spectacle usually lasts for about a week, and at its height there can be more than 300 frogs in the garden, with the noise continuing both day and night. However, at the slightest movement within the vicinity of the pond, all goes quiet as the frogs sink below the surface.

During mating, the male frog will grip hold of the female from behind – a position known as amplexus.

Carnivores Of The Deep

O n a warm, sunny evening, the garden pond appears to be a tranquil place; plants wave in the breeze and insects hum round the flowers. But, as the saying goes, beauty is only skin deep; under the surface is a very different world. It is a world where nature rules and the fittest survive by relying on speed, stealth, or camouflage, and a deadly sting or powerful jaws are a distinct advantage.

War In The Water

It is not difficult to enter this world: simply move closer to the water, select a comfortable position where the water is clear and the bottom visible, and sit still. Three-spined sticklebacks can be seen moving in and out of the weed as they hunt for newt larva, freshwater shrimps, or any other small creature they can swallow. The male is easily recognisable in his bright-red breeding colours. A shoal of young sticklebacks swim into the weed, unaware that danger lurks within.

The three-spined stickleback will hunt any creature that it can swallow!

A three-spined stickleback attacks a minnow approaching its nest.

Waiting motionless, superbly camouflaged, as it hangs on to the weed is the greenish-brown water stick insect – poised, mantis-like, ready to strike. A fish swims too close, and the water stick insect strikes, grasping the fish with its specially-adapted front legs, which draw the fish in and on to the sharp rostrum.

Dragonfly Nymphs

Equally at home in the waterweed are the dragonfly nymphs, which, in the case of the emperor or southern hawker, may be nearly 2.4 ins (6 cms) long. Usually green or brown in colour, they move slowly though the water and do not need to surface because they can extract oxygen from the water by passing it through the abdominal cavity.

The feature which makes the dragonfly nymph such a formidable predator is its unique hinged mask, which terminates in a pair of large pincers. When prey, such as a tadpole, moves within striking distance, the mask moves upwards and outwards with lightning speed to grasp the prey with the pincers, which then bring it into the nymph's powerful jaws.

Tadpoles are no match for the formidable emperor dragonfly nymph.

Carnivores Of The Deep

Prowling Tigers

Out of the gloom, weaving its way through the waterweed comes a large, brown streamlined beetle, using its back legs, which are fringed with hairs, to propel it through the water in its unrelenting search for food. It's a female great diving beetle with dark-brown ridged wing cases and a distinctive light-brown band round the body and head. The male has a smooth body and the ridging is absent.

Suddenly it stops swimming and floats slowly to the surface. The tip of the abdomen breaks through the surface as it takes in air. The air is carried as a bubble under the wing cases, which makes it naturally buoyant, so it must either swim or hold on to the water weed, using its hooked front feet.

It swims downwards and anchors itself to the waterweed. Staying motionless, it waits. It is a fearless hunter, often attacking pond creatures much larger than itself. Using its large pale blue eyes, it spots the stickleback as it moves

The great diving beetle constantly hunts the pond in search of food.

slowly through the water below. Unaware of the danger above, the stickleback moves closer.

All at once, the diving beetle propels itself forwards, and, using its powerful legs, grasps the stickleback. A brief struggle ensues before the beetle settles down to feed using its large mandibles to tear up the prey before swallowing the pieces.

A pair of great diving beetles make a fierce team. Here, they are eating a young golden orfe.

Water Tigers

Fierce the adult may be, but it is the beetle larva which are the truly fearsome hunters. Growing to a length of 2.4 ins (6 cms) they swim slowly but fearlessly through the water, using their six legs as paddles. The larva floats tail-first to the surface to take in air, and then it swims down and anchors itself to a waterweed and waits with its body in the characteristic arched position.

A tadpole swims by, and the larva strikes, propelling itself forwards with lightning speed to grasp its prey with its large pincer-like mandibles.

These are the ultimate design in feeding technique – not only do they hold the prey in a vice-like grip, but they are hollow, to allow the digestive juices to be pumped into the prey and the contents sucked out like a soup to leave an empty shell.

No wonder frogs and newts lay so many eggs – with such efficient predators, only a few manage to survive to maturity.

Sticklebacks And Newts

If you have an interest in ponds, then you have probably seen a stickleback. The male three-spined stickleback in full breeding colours is a pugnacious brightly-coloured little fish that would not look out of place in a tropical fish aquarium. The belly and chin take on a bright red colour and the back becomes a steely blue-grey, which is complemented by the piercing blue colour of its large eyes.

The three-spined stickleback is a spectacular, brightly-coloured fish.

Setting Boundaries

Having selected a territory, he excavates a pit on the pond bottom. He then collects fragments of vegetation, which he forms into a mound, glued together with a secretion from his kidneys. He makes a tunnel through the mound, and tries to entice pregnant females into the tunnel to spawn.

Over a period of days, a successful male will persuade several females to lay their eggs in his nest. He then drives the females away and assumes total responsibility for the eggs, guarding them against predators and ensuring they receive enough oxygen by fanning currents of water over them. When they hatch, he continues to look after the fry by keeping them together in a small shoal.

These interesting little fish and their close relative, the nine-spined stickleback, are an asset to any pond. However, they

The ten-spined stickleback, like its cousins, is extremely territorial. Here, a male is guarding a nest of eggs.

are extremely territorial, and, if you keep sticklebacks, then you will not have any newts in the pond. This is because, over a few years, they will eat the young newts and drive the adults away.

Now For The Good Newts...

There are three species of newts in this country. The common or smooth newt is frequently found in ponds, performing its courtship ritual in early spring.

Palmate newts are more common in the west, and, if you are lucky, your pond could become home to a colony of great-crested newts. Approaching six inches in length, these newts are unmistakable with their warty black skin and bright orange underbelly. In full breeding condition the male develops a large crest along his back and down the top of his tail.

Newts are active in the pond from March through to July, and the best time to view them is at night with the aid of a torch. Moving into shallow water, the female walks along the bottom, with the male in attendance. He stops in front of her and waves his tail to create a current of water to court her.

Great-crested newts, in particular, love to hang in the open water between the patches of weed, where they can be easily picked up in the torch beam.

Smooth newts start courting in early spring.

The unmistakable great-crested newt is a protected species.

23

In The Air

Often, we are attracted to the pond not by what's in the water but by what's happening in the air above the pond. On a warm day in July the pond becomes a hive of activity because many of the creatures found below the water spend their short adult lives in the air.

From his vantage point on a reedmace or branch, the emperor dragonfly (our largest dragonfly species) defends his territory, launching himself into the air to repel invaders.

Southern hawkers are inquisitive, rather tame insects that lay their eggs at the edges of ponds.

Southern hawkers lay their eggs round the edge of the pond and are quite tame, inquisitive even, approaching to within a foot or so if you stand quietly at the edge of the pond. Even a small pond may attract several pairs of common darters, smaller dragonflies which fly in tandem, the brown-bodied female laying her eggs below the water, grasped from above by the red-bodied male.

Damsels And Demoiselles

Delicate damselflies dance in and out of the sedges, hunting for small flies; once paired, they rest on the lily pads between frantic bouts of egg-laying. As

Demoiselles are considerably larger than damselflies. Pictured: a male banded demoiselle.

many as five species of damselfly may be seen round the garden pond together, with two species of demoiselle.

The demoiselles are much larger, with wide brightly-coloured wings and a metallic sheen to their bodies. The male banded demoiselle has a violet patch on each wing, truly magnificent insects as they catch the rays of the setting sun.

A pair of large red damselflies.

May Day

When conditions are right, the air above the pond can become alive with activity. Mayflies, there are many different species, can all hatch within a few minutes of each other. Timing is essential because the adult will only live for a day, mating and laying its eggs before it dies.

Adult mayflies live only for one day. Pictured: a newly-hatched mayfly near to its recently-cast skin.

DID YOU KNOW?

The dragonfly can catch and eat its prey on the wing, by using its legs to form a cradle.

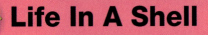

Ramshorn snails feed off pond algae.

DID YOU KNOW?

Snails are more common where the water contains calcium, which is used to make their shells.

Many soft-bodied creatures are successful inhabitants of the pond because they have the benefit of a hard shell to protect them. Most obvious are the water snails, particularly the great pond snail with its conical pointed shell.

Given the right conditions, these snails breed rapidly and can munch their way through lots of tender water plants, becoming too plentiful in some instances. If you are lucky, the chocolate-brown ramshorn snail may live in the pond. Approaching an inch (2.5 cms) in diameter, these delicate snails are a positive asset, feeding on algae.

Swan Mussels

Freshwater mussels, such as the large swan mussel, can live in the pond, providing the water quality is good. They live on the bottom, taking in a continuous stream of water from which they filter food particles and oxygen. These large molluscs are sometimes sold as a cure for a dirty pond, but they are unlikely to survive and will die, simply adding to the problem.

Natural Protection

The caddis fly is a fairly uninteresting moth-like fly, but its larva or grub has developed a very neat protective case by sticking together material it finds in the pond. Each species uses different material to make a distinctive case. Some roll dead leaves, almost like making a cigar, while others utilise small pebbles or even small pieces of twig. This hard shell allows the caddis grub to graze on pond plants in relative safety.

Another interesting creature is the caterpillar of the china mark moth which makes a protective case out of two pieces of water lily leaf. These are cut as neat semicircles from the edge of the leaf and then glued together to form an envelope which will float on the surface.

The caterpillar of the china mark moth constructs a floating protective case from a water lily.

I t is not only plants which are threatening to take over the pond. Over the years, animals have also gained a foothold in our countryside. Marsh frogs are firmly established in the south of England, where, given time, they may displace our native common frogs, as they compete for food and habitat. The midwife toad, which actually carries its eggs on its back, has established a small colony in Bedfordshire, but it is the bullfrog, terrapins and turtles that pose the largest threat because of their predatory nature.

Bullfrogs, residents of the United States, are already established in some of the warmer parts of Europe, and, in recent years, have managed to survive in the wild in this country. In the 1990s, many tadpoles were imported and released into garden ponds where they grew apace, often reaching a length of 5 inches (12.5 cms) before starting

DID YOU KNOW?

The freshwater mussel allows the bitterling (below) to lay its eggs inside its shell for protection. In return, when the tiny bitterlings leave the shell, they take the baby mussels with them.

Bitterling and fresh water mussel.

to turn into frogs. Eating anything they can swallow, Bullfrogs will soon clear a pond of small native aquatic creatures, and, over the next few years, develop

Red-eared terrapin sliding into water.

into frogs as large as dinner plates. Adult frogs are living from year to year in the wild, although there is no evidence that they are breeding.

Fearsome Ninjas

Remember the Ninja turtle craze of the early 90s? Many of those tiny, must-have, red-eared terrapins, are now full grown and well established in our ponds and lakes. They grew quickly in captivity and many were released into lakes in local parks where they have grown into fearsome predators capable of catching and eating most of our native amphibians and reptiles.

Less common, but even larger, is the snapper turtle, which may grow to nearly 2 feet (60 cms) in length and is capable of eating even the larger fish. Again, fortunately, none of these creatures have managed to breed. However, with increases in temperature, the potential is there, particularly in the south.

Snapper turtles, together with other 'aliens', wreak havoc on native pond wildlife.

After Dark

As the sun sets and the temperatures fall, dragonflies and damselflies move to the pondside vegetation to rest for the night, and gradually all becomes quiet. In the twilight, pipestrelle bats fly, dipping low over the pond to take mayflies, as they dance above the water.

DID YOU KNOW?

It is an offence to release alien species into a garden pond because of the damage they can cause to native creatures.

Night Activity

As darkness falls, the amphibians, now protected from the hot rays of the sun, move out to feed. The common toad, from a hole in a log near the pond, walks slowly through the undergrowth, taking small slugs from the leaves and worms from the ground. His appetite is almost insatiable.

The grass snake enjoys an occasional dip in the garden pond.

Shine a torch across the pond. Frogs hang in the water with just their heads showing through the pond plants, or sit motionless on a lilypad, waiting for a fly to move within range of their long sticky tongues.

Newts hang motionless in the water as a grass snake swims, head weaving from side to side and tongue flicking in and out as it tastes the air in its search for frogs.

A New Dawn

A family of hedgehogs move along the border, stopping to drink from the pond, and, just before dawn breaks, a heron drops silently out of the sky and walks across the lawn to the edge of the pond. He waits motionless, a frog moves, the heron strikes and another meal is secured and he leaves to feed his hungry youngsters. But he will be back, as life ebbs and flows in the garden pond.

With a healthy food chain established, a successful pond can attract larger animals, such as the hedgehog.